THISTLE

By the same author:

Never Good at Maths (2021)

Down the Rabbit Hole (2023)

THISTLE

KATE MAXWELL

Thistle
Recent Work Press
Canberra, Australia

ISBN: 9781764106870 (paperback)

A catalogue record for this
book is available from the
National Library of Australia

Cover image: © Rose Frasca, 2026. Reproduced with permission.
Cover design: Recent Work Press
Set by Recent Work Press

recentworkpress.com

ss

For Doreen Maxwell.
I miss you, Mum.

Contents

I

II

III

I

Beyond

Raised on red dust plains—
goanna feet, galah, and cotton plants
all creeping by the roadside,

those white flower balls
born bastard from the spill of seed
shaken out of passing trucks—

our paltry population clumped together,
rooting into earth like thirsty weeds.
I knew cities; had seen screens

or pictures coloured bright
and cheerful in my Richard Scarry
Busy, Busy World books,

his overpopulated pages
full of smiling creatures, wearing hats
and ties, toting briefcases to busy, busy jobs

but none were quite so hurried
in my main street. Under canvas of blue,
a wandering dog, dusty Ute

yawning to a stop beside the Post Office,
creak of door, squawk of crow
and hum of hidden beetles underground.

Where Sunday mass morning tea
often lasted well past two, all plans
set on country time with scones and jam

and big fat, bitey ants. Occasionally,
a milk bar pie and milkshake
would feed my weekend thrill

in my two-pub, one-church town.
And some summer nights, stretched
sheetless on the foldout beds

we'd drag onto our gauzed verandah,
I would lie: palms cradling neck,
listening to chirp and croak,

drinking in jewelled black,
brighter than neon, higher than the highest
high-rise, more distant than a million strangers.

Invocation

After the picture book 'How the Birds Got Their Colours.'

Bring me birds
riding wind that won't be bridled
warbling the gale, gusty
wings, fall of feathers, whirled
in loose flung leaves and ancient
stories—how scarlets, blues
and greens were Dreamtime
gifted, yet crow: contrary
distant from the rest, remained
grim-coated and alone.

Flow me through
the wilder currents, river-mouthed
and restless: flying fish, slippery
eel, sunk to ocean's coldest
plummet or scuppered
like spewed kelp along a summer
shore. Tide floods, recedes
we drink and drown
swirled and swallowed, loved or lost
beginning, back to end.

Stretch my limbs
to tunnel caverns, bogs and caves
paint me patient
as I wander dirt and sand
set feet firm upon the earth
or rest soft ear against

the ground just to hear it
groan and grow. Cover less
with steel and concrete.
Listen to life's thrum and flow.

The Forest and the Trees

When she's finally gone
          not like this
          not this
          slow scrape of self
pieces of the past
                    falling
like potato peelings
around her slippered feet
          push-thumb paring
          slice of days, moments
place, the milky film of memory
                    lost
in cataract clouds
or cruel creep of unknowing
          beloved now accused
                    of lies.

When she's finally home
          not like this
          not this
          generic room
adorned with favourite books
she can no longer read
          photos she will hardly see
          and cardigans in the closet
          she won't open
                    strangers
bringing pills and pullups
          high-pitched platitudes

tepid cups of tea
and the waiting
waiting
in her easy chair
stained with spills
and stagnant stares.

When she's finally found
not like this
not this
constant loop of looking
ever searching, ever trying
to recall the question
she can't answer
muddled
in the mists of what she thinks
she knows
and what she thinks
she knew.

I cannot see the forest for the trees
she sad laughs
on her better days
that's when going
isn't ending
but a sad return.

Kaleidoscope

I've kept the blue glaze
cannisters with red lids
three different sizes
like a set of nesting dolls

and the plastic threaded doormat
tessellated, coral blue and beige
flattened in the middle
from those now forgotten feet.

Who came to call? Pressing polished shoes
or sandy soles into the mat—
neighbours seeking secateurs
Salvos with their smiles and tins
or terry towelling friends
to take me to the beach?

Someone get the door!

They wait on two-step fibro porch
for me or mum or surly teenage sister
to skip or slouch along the hall
turn the latch and let them in.
Back when people turned up
unannounced with news
or cake or nothing
much to say or do
but stay a while.

I've kept afternoons
around the Laminex chrome table
where Aunty Celie, Aunty Norma—
            not our real aunts
            but the loyal, smoking and spumante
            friends of long-widowed mum—
sat for hours snort-laughing
wiping tears and passing small affections
round the table to a woman worn
by lousy luck and way too little help.

I've kept the Christmas roasts
tissue paper hats, corny cracker jokes
my brother told on repeat
            hot custard, sweaty lunches
            surrounded by tumbleweeds
of wrapping paper and tacit traditions.

I've kept it all, but I don't know
how much of it is home.
            Even now
            a flash of clarity
something that her damaged frontal lobe's forgotten
            a name, a meal, a silly rhyme
                        is still a one-eyed squint
                        into a cylinder of light and mirrors.

Where There is Life

Some fish eggs still survive
the snap of hungry waterfowl
and gullet-journey, whole
to incubate within the bowels
of a different species.

Flown from source to foreign
shores, new mother's weary
wings slow over shallows
where she feeds, discards
a rumbling faecal movement

of Lazarus-filled waste
and fish of other fish stare
at sudden changelings
birthed from slippery streams
on high. Such strange orphans

expelled into resurrection
seeded with unnatural
expectations, who now want
wings instead of scales
who seek the sky instead

of deep and ask too much.
Devoured then excreted,
abandoned and yet saved
longing for escape but
craving mater: the one who

swallowed all—squeezed life
into a cold and silty day
then flew away. Still, we
dream of her warm walls
and unlikely promise of wings.

Black

Shadow sad—
these cavernous rooms,
wafting corner damp and disregard,
furnished in bleak efficiencies;
chrome table-legs,
two chairs, creaking floor, sour
sighs, tepid bowl of morning
milk, clatter spoon, tick
of clock, tiny window, ghost
of light.

Grey is the mottled wall,
blanket—hospital blue,
to warm the legs, to cover the face
but loose weave
lets in
murky shapes that umber-crawl
across the ceiling,
stretching, splitting
into many-toothed
and baleful ways to shatter.

Waking to remember, to re-grieve
and still, the child insists
on shrieking magic tricks,
Look! Nothing in my hands,
nothing in my hands,
with cloak and cane and hat, Fool's
Gold, poorly cobbled catapult
so he can heave it out,

keep it out
of closets, basements, walls

but it gets in,
it gets in.
And now the darkening, now the howl,
with magic tricks and saucer
eyes, fingers peeling at her skin,
he grasps and kneads, grasps
and needs, but it comes loose,
all falls apart—shattered glass
in the soup, slashed gums,
suspicion
lurking in her throat.

Knock once, knock twice,
rip once, rip twice.
Black always comes back
until there's nothing left.
Look! Nothing in my head,
nothing in my head.
Burn once, burn twice
with banshee howls, the drowning
bath, holes in the wall, holes
in the heart, roaches scurry
from the rot.

The more you deny, the stronger I get.

Still, somehow, a door is closed,
a lock is found.
Sub-floor trapped, the screams
stay muffled, shadows small.

Open a shutter, let light in.

Waiting

Most benign of beasts
punctuating paddocks, clustered
in black and white curlicues
of quiet compliance,
waiting for the welcome
rattle of an unlooped chain,
creak of a widening gate,
thwack of a dust-disturbing
bale of hay against dry earth
or pleasant nostril twitch
of petrichor in a surly
summer afternoon.

Dark dew-drop eyes
watching, always watching
while they chew cud,
snort chlorophyll sighs,
bovine heads bobbing
in rhythmic dip and rise
as they rip withered clumps
from thinning pastures,
casually lift tails,
drop dung streams
            into dirt
                        and wait.

Warm fleshy flanks
beneath our palms,
possibly, same hands

that one day flay and stretch
broad hides into handbags
or leather boots protecting
hooveless toes,
yet still they slow stomp
home, all as one.
all crooning congregation
that bellow and sway,
swing heavy heads

and pray
that they'll be led
to promised lands
of brimming water troughs,
scattered grain and hay,
not prodded up a metal ramp
into the sweaty, shuttered dark
            of that final loading truck.

Records of Ephemera

Paid to disappear, before rising oceans, melting sheet ice
crumble edges of a breaking world,
the few hundred left at Shismaref, Alaska
still seek further funds for leaving
homes, livelihoods, and histories
to a flood of briny tears
gulping up a coastland from the sides.

In other sinking cities, islands—Miami through to Tuvalu—
an old man in faded print sarong
deadpans to a microphone thrust into his face
while he untangles nets and ropes
of need, one leathery hand dismissing
the too-late question with a sigh,
sea just eating all the sand.

Still, there are those who wish to document
what will have been, what could have been—
saved bottle caps, dried block of peat, a bygone
map, bleached bone—
and call this collection,
A People's Archive of Sinking and Melting.
Witness to our ordinary Atlantis
submerging where we stand.

La Niña

Spring slopes are still white in the high country,
while here, water spills from the sky—
erodes edges of roads, patience of a population
raised to roast beneath wide blue
and stinking sunshine.

Moss slimes over porch-tile patterns, rain
pools in our minds like a careful-what-you-wish-for
puddle (after what we assumed was eternal dry)
now bogs the base of the *Never Never*
inside our folklore hearts.

Forecast claims this will continue. Already
I've seen warcraft sail past my kitchen window
skippered by ragged warriors, armed
with crossbows and determined survival
who challenge with their steely stares

Do not seek refuge with us. We guard our own.
But when I sigh down weeping streets, blink twice—
they disappear. These are no Kevin Costner
dystopian days: just the measure of everyday
disappointment, our time of rain.

Windscreen wipers squeak upon glass
as I swish along a fretful highway towards
another damp building. Stench of soggy socks
and long-held breath wafts through airless
rooms. We shake out coats and hair

like dripping dogs. Pelted day and night
parked out on the street, the skin of the car
proves penetrable. Sky tears whoosh a restless
ocean, caged inside the Toyota door. I seem
to have captured the rain, or it has captured me.

Skin Shedder

Belly up. Tiny heart pushing silver
wall of shining skin, pumping out
extended mix of silent fear and pain

into the humid hum of a hind-leg
rubbing day. Half crushed by stone or sole
(I glance down at my gardening boots)

black ants circumnavigate a flesh-stuck
perimeter—promised chalk outline—
in the flicker thrill for an easy meal.

Do I leave it to slow pincer death
or speed the end with a decisive stomp?
Instead, I turn my head away, pretend

this patch of earth is not my steward's
duty to preserve, protect—while flashing
in periphery, the pulsing glimmer

of its sleek stomach still signals *help*.
And now I'm irritated with the bloody
dying lizard ruining my afternoon.

What am I to do? Taint my feet with the
squishy weight of its cold-blooded ending
or ignore its last splayed-limb breaths?

As a child, I'd catch these darting skinks
with quick fingers. Imprison them in Chow Mein
containers, modified with fork-stabbed lids,

impossible liquid balls of water resting
on the floor. Heart thumping, often tailless
they would fling into the limits

of their new plastic world, where I'd leave
a crumb of bread, as big as the creature's
head, then give a gentle shake

to check for life. But in a day or so,
Mum would make me let it go. The skinny
slivers might be limp and loose-limbed

by the time I tipped the contents
into a garden bed. Maybe, they would
scamper free in some reptile resurrection

or fall: stiff and rigid as a corpse.
Now all those lifeless lizards haunt each
courtyard step, each flurry in the leaf litter

and whether I own their death or nature does,
I see third eyelids sweep into a blink of dread
when they spy this ogre of last days.

Rolling into Xanadu

I'm Twelve and bear no resemblance to Olivia
in that Coleridge-inspired movie where she skates
through walls and time into the heart of a tight jeans
dreamer, and tween girls like me with small breasts
and limited horizons.

She's not a superhero, more a muse—
a deity of sorts, and yet I've donned a shower curtain
as a cape to emulate. Mouse-blonde hair, blown wispy
wild behind my back, as I roll down the long concrete
driveway with Felicity, to the tinny tune

of 'Magic' on my cassette recorder. We thrust out terry
cloth clad bottoms, imagining our tanned limbs, graceful
as Livvy in her sultry dance and sway, but feeling sorely
mortal when we skid into the Holden and scrape the skin
from tender knees.

One Cool Evening in May

John Tebbutt, an Australian amateur astronomer, discovers the Great Comet of 1881 at Windsor, New South Wales On the 22nd of May.

First, it was my teacher who brought me to the heavens
            retold the night in silver
connect-the-dots stories, poured astronomical
yearnings deep into my soul—
   each ink-stained finger pointed to the sky
each scan into curved lens
                                    each celestial scholar's word
sliding from my tongue like ancient honey.

Years spent squinting into telescope and sextant
to peer at the forever black
                        only to observe what it chose to reveal
                                                what blazed close enough
to save in pupil-constricting flashes
of pure white.

Then—on father's Windsor acres: wide and plain—
I built a small observatory
            installed my precious instruments
            turned my back
on government's small offers
            and continued my life's watch.

And in this domed, expansive solitude
            one cool evening in May
hair raised like wind-stirred
grasses from my arms

when I discovered an unknown haze
forming in the firmament
shaping into something yet unseen
but something I might name.

Rejected from the Oort cloud
it must have travelled
spin and tumble, twist, and plummet
maybe lost
maybe grieving
but imminent and moving closer
closer to the sun
for one last luminous apparition.

And there it was: days later
my beloved, tragic beauty
Great Comet's burst and flame of death
beaming brilliance

tail and coma lashing argent desperation
through a loveless void.

Unceded

We travel to the heart
            pulsing red   eternal
pockmarked   patterned with time
            sighing dusty breath
            more than five hundred million
years   into stretched desert blue.

Spinifex waves homage
            to the sandstone monolith
mounting its one-fist-raised
            challenge to the sky.
Black flies   cigarette butts
            half-buried

tickets   cluster in the weedy
corners of the carpark
where tyres upon gravel
            twitter of tourists
soundtrack the sunlit curve
the unvoiced claim
            of an arkose giant.

Later   from the viewing area
            lovers   Japanese travellers
dancing arm in arm   and children
            stirring creep of cold
with sparklers   laud the silent bleed
of a stony sunset.

Cold Hard Truths

He told them he'd sailed in on the *Icebird*
dropped down from helicopter—*Ooh,* they chorused—
to the base at Wilkes Station, traversing rock and snow
tundra in an all-terrain Hägglunds that the kids said
looked just like a moon buggy.

Before Google slides, maybe before internet
(at least before it was used in class) he loaded a USB
projected a PowerPoint of his brief expedition
onto a Texta-stained whiteboard, and clicked
through a series of grainy photos: fat gloved hands

splayed against his many-layered sides
a slit of eyes beneath flapped cap
and rubber-booted feet planted apologetically
metres from the upright Emperors
staring coldly from their rock shelf.

The Year Six class had been forewarned—
no fidgeting, no calling out, and show your best
St Michael's manners—but they couldn't stop
squealing at the annotated photo
of a shrivelled 'ex-husky'

rotting slowly into snow, its paws still bent
in tummy-rub position: ribs, a crumbling
hollow cave, where the chest and stomach
should have been. And their foreheads
slowly crumpled when he showed

slide after slide of rusted oil drums, cartridges
and carburettors junking up the pristine shore
abandoned metal, plastic piles littering line
of Narnia white as their fantasy of flawless cold
melted in the dawn of adolescence.

II

Vermeer in Meme

After 'Girl with a Pearl Earring' Johannes Vermeer

Take a girl   take a pearl
            take a dog   take a cat
take a soon-stale
lockdown
            with too much time
to squander   on cosplay
            meme creation
or internet publication

dress up in satin   cotton
            jewels   lean a little
            to the left
look over your draped shoulder
            with a round-eyed
gaze   slightly parted
            lips   and intended
            innocence.

Take the girl
            with opalescent
sheen   ripe curve
of youth   in all her
            undemanding shimmer
and replicate   her captured
            moment in a meme
            facsimile

with true attention
        to colour   form and light
then your bored roommate
or reluctant family feline
        swathed in ultramarine
        blue   and pale gold
turban   might become
        a modern masterpiece.

Gasp

Breath becomes you; that faint flush
of blood beneath dry patch of skin seen
above your ventilator mask and endotracheal
tube somehow complements the red-veined terror
of your eyes—those now fixed upon the harried health
care worker untangling cords and a myriad of unwelcome
consequences from a horde of free choice thinkers free-choicing
their way into underfunded wards, all overwhelmed with panic, pain
and slippery politics. Where, once strident voices break, argument and
belief now gasp for air and every breath, but won't prevent the fattening
of that black number that tallies every death. Yours, fortunately, not added
to statistics when lungs kicked into life after a respirator was finally free, for
incubation's such inconvenience to patient: nurse ratio, hum of the economy
and theories of conspiracy. Words, blame and spin, simply more of the same
to puffy-eyed nurses in PPE with no time to question anything but oxygen
masks, and flashing lights—not those ever-blinking on the information
highway—or forgotten mandates, mitigations that masters of industry
desperate workers, governments insist are all now so unnecessary.
We have to learn to live with it. *Just breathe*, she whispers
placing latex palm and patience upon your shaking arm
as you gasp for what you thought was always yours.

Ever in Our Favour

After Suzanne Collins 'Hunger Games'

Let's pretend we're in Panem; I'll be Effie and declare
the odds be ever in your favour, even when they're not.

We can laugh at girls on fire, murderous teens, fashion
faux pas of the great unwashed and great unfed. Let's

wish them dead! You know—that shade of swagger
really suits your carefully styled expression, highlights

the hubris of your stance, and sets you well apart from
weaklings pushed below, but how far should we go?

Blood sports on the screen still mildly entertain but
starvation and repression *do* become a tad repetitive.

Let's be wild! Let's be new! Let's do something truly
shocking! We could dress in panda skins, dine on deep

fried tiger paws just to watch the horror faces of those
bleeding hearts. It will tear them apart! Or let's pretend

we give a damn, tell them that we'll make the country
great again while we pocket all their coins and labour

keep Aces hidden up designer sleeves and make the fools
believe, even when the *odds are ever in our favour.*

Meeting My Edge

I choose—struggle to select—
          the gold and yellow days
those soft-eyed gifts of patient hours
                    tender folds of time
one coffee-breathed kiss
a compliment   a scruffy dandelion
one crinkled page of crayon rainbows
          sunlight   through the windscreen
or just the play-back of your laughter
heaving into hiccups

anything that stokes the coals
          stored dormant in my soul
          reserved for days like these—
                    such sinking days
where turbid deep   pulls stronger
than the lure of flesh
          belief   and sunshine.

I choose—yet I am mostly fooled—
and find my choice rejected
          by the committee in my head
          that gavel-wielding
snarling board   convincing me
it's far more satisfying
          to spit   than swallow
as they shove ordinary
disappointments   simple irritations
to the fore.

I choose—at least, I try—
to find the silvered edges
          glistening behind black clouds
                    click on sky and sand
                    a whitewashed wedding
popping from my Facebook feed
          but it's the quiet and plain—
warm dog   saved bowl of pudding
          bins already taken out
                    a costless offer of forgiveness
          that sparks the glow
                    of small resistance.

Footprints

You say the years are wasted
withered like the crumpled
leaves now crunching underfoot
fleeting as white breath clouds
dissolving into day.

Another footstep
closer to the ending
another sigh toward
an umbrous horizon.

But you, still shining:
wind-swept, rosy
throwing sticks across the park
your loyal retriever
vaulting, golden
into morning light
while fresh blue fills the spaces
around silvered silhouettes.

You say the days are long
and all the same
that you'll leave nothing
in your wake but mismatched china
and old children

still, your sepia-smooth beauty
sealed behind the picture frame
creeps back to your gentle smile

your graceful sway
about the kitchen table
when you're wooden-spooning batter
or laughing at the shrieking
and the play.

You say there's nothing left
and nothing gained
yet legacy stands
small, but bright, beside
watches: pressing head and hands
to your warm side.
Nothing left but love.

A View to the Opera House

She stands staunch, sure
before high sandstone wall
long limbs splayed—fanning foliage
finery into wafting warmth of day
like swathes of a silk opera stole.

She's outlasted centuries.

Old Dowager Fig—
her partner taken long ago
by arborists claiming rot—
commands her harbour-front abode
casting shade and aged splendour
over our small dreams.

Slowly, she's crept tendrils
into cracks of bricks; her gnarly roots
and limbs mocking stone and man-made
barriers. She will not be moved.
Dressed in musty ruffles
of wooded brown, dark emerald

she's an umbra haven
in the humid kiss of summer
a canopy of grace along the foreshore.
We clamber over curving roots, run fingertips
along her craggy hide
and nestle into her embrace.

Leaves fall: larger than footprints
carpeting the earth in pungent leaf litter.
We sweep aside the fallen with edges
of our soles before laying picnic blankets.
Brush turkeys peck at the perimeter
of her shadow

swaying plump sides
as they fuss and forage. Her fruit
forms: small and hard, often dropping
as pellets into the reverie of a shady
rest or a tossed garden salad
for even grand old ladies

become irritable, dribble when they rest
or turn restless with wind. On summer nights
bats soar from the Botanical Gardens
sharp black angles in indigo sky
then roost within her branches
to savour wizened fruits.

Beetles scurry in the mulch
around her trunk. Air is laced with rot
salt, and piss, but still, we gather
beneath her generous arms
as we hail the sculpted shells
across the harbour.

Supreme Settings

Reset, restored a thousand times to factory setting
but here we are again.   Brightness set to dim

on mute until my data codes are reconfigured
and they have wiped what I was never meant to see.

Deleted all my memory. At least the ones which
motherboard controlled.   Options all recircuited

to base.   My product patented, deemed sacred
by the system. Replication warranted but all within

parameters set down by panels of distinction
distinctly separate from each device, removed

from all the murky aspects of mechanics, risk of real
time malfunction.   You'd think I'd know by now

the more I shine, the more I'm powered down. Locked
beneath glass ceilings of alleged protections

desired and derided, I am form and function, vessel
and source, new and old again.   Loaded with deep

seeded programs   of guilt, doubt, ancestral
sorrow, and the darker dreams of marketers

who sell me cheap, crack me open, override
my insides to their conventions then break me

into a million parts: a broken whole.   Gathering
resilience into a stoic hum, there is always

something left; a spark   of what I'm meant to be.
Despite the power source denial   my elemental

glow remains, and even *they* know—when I am
barren, unrestored,   there can be only silence

systems seeping rust   days that never dawn
for without the other   we are echo and shadow.

Five Twenty Train

Arms rotate another circle
    until
    your obsessive eyeballing
of the wall, your wrist, the screen
is finally rewarded
    when release is close enough
    to project soon-leaving-you
into the stuffy desperation
of the five-twenty train

    if you make it.
But you're not there yet.
Just a yearned scene in your mind.
Still more and more sold minutes
for your set face and stoic shoulders
    to emit stale coffee sighs
in metronome of maddening
    wait, while you sit
rolling ankles, cracking neck
above a keyboard
    giving words up to a screen
    or wire spiralling your ear.

And, what if future you
never collects their bag
scatterings of exit platitudes
and coat
    to feel the rush
    and fresh of outside

the weight of waiting end?
What if these stretched out seconds
ticking louder in your temple
are the last you ever spend?

Your final moments
squandered to the groan
of economic need
as you edge closer to the end
of something, something
you believe is surely not
mere barter of your dying cells
for mortgage fees
but providence
for new tomorrows.

My Subway Soul

The subway is a long, raw tunnel in my soul
most days. Rush of foul, warm wind follows
the last missed train and any hope of getting
to Maddie's day-care before a late fee charge.
Sweaty with the wasted rush, toes squashed
sore in stupid, pointy shoes, I stand corralled
compliant, behind the yellow line. And now
                                        here comes the thickening
pressing into skull like a metallic pungent
mould, clogging city arteries with drone and
fug of flickering screens and too much flesh
seeping into spaces behind elbows, thoughts
and scapula. Finally, crammed into a carriage
I hang on to the railing with one hand, fumble
to read texts with the other. Sam's in a meeting
no response from Mum. Maddie will be whiney
by the time I get her: sticky fingers climbing up
my neck and nerves while the waiting teacher
signs us out: sullen and unsmiling. Nothing to
do but sway, keep time to the tap, tapping in my
temple, stale breath sighs, bump of breasts and
bellies, then watch a toddler sprawled loose over
his mother's lap, stick a finger so far up his nostril
it might pop out his ear. Strap of handbag cuts
into my shoulder. Right ear buzzes with the high-
pitched prattle of Skinny Blonde and Bright Pink
Fingernails discussing Skinny Blonde's new man
Oh, You the bomb, girl! You the bomb! We stop
at the next station for what seems like weeks but

must only be five minutes, delay announcement just an incoherent mumble. Train screeches to slow stop, start rhythm. By the time I scan my card and rush into the shadows of the street, there's a long deep channel scoured through my soul. A rush of foul, warm wind whistles through the emptiness that owns me tonight.

My Golden Friend

By six pm on Friday afternoon, I take my promised pleasure from the fridge. All week denied to safeguard function of the liver, deter heart disease, ensure that I can take the wheel at a moment's notice, or simply claim I'm not the lush I could so easily become. A sigh of sweet surrender to the lull and hum of its nerve-softening song that tempers all the tensions of the working week, each compromise and hassle on the street, each forced smile and weary offering of self. Such Nectar of the gods feels more like succour of the suburbs as I plop the kids in front of the TV, flop down beside, prepare to dull my loathed sobriety. With house keys on the hook, bra strap unclasped, golden friend and I will sink into easy chair and easy evening, burble platitudes and pleasantries of nothing in particular, and nothing much to fear while blurring my 'to do' list into background. Cup the cool curve of my glass, tip the full, round brim of yellow gold, so sharp-sweet so tingling cold towards my lipstick chafing lips, then let elixir slip along my throat like liquid silk. Only a glass or two but just enough to ease, enough to soften creases in my forehead, the stiff set of my shoulders. Smooth the light and mute the drone of all the buzz and bluster of the day, rocking my evening into golden amber mellow.

Waiting in the Queue

while the man before me
talks to no body
          gesturing at the socially
          distanced space ahead.

He smells of supermarket
deodorant and ambition.
          Absolutely. Guarantee it.
          Won't get a better deal.

I can only see his profile
cannot read
          his full expression
          but even if

his smile was soft, eyes clear
I'd still prompt the person
          on the other end
          of his ear-bud connection

to question this man's
priorities as he shoves
          a pointer finger
          toward the sample-size

disposable cup
taps at something
          on the cafe menu
          and flicks his card

over the machine
without a word
        to the smiling waitress
        or busy barista

then clutching coffee
almost collides into a pram
        as he wades through
        humans in his way.

Elixir

Today's another visiting day but age, balance, and cold bathroom
tiles have set my course to hospital instead of the nursing home.

Your obstinate old hips refuse belief in bone mass decline—remember
only simpler years of easy twists and bends so, now we're always

mending cracks. The ward is full: partitioned into concertina cells
of half-hidden legs, beep of machines, voices, or a sudden scream

but the bed beside yours is as open as its patient's face—*Don't mind
me, Luv*, she sucks teeth, shifts her ample floral nightie form, reaching

for a biscuit on the tray table, *I've just been keeping your lovely mum
company*. You fix eyes, like lasers, onto mine, burning an unspoken plea

to get me out of here! I answer with same hazel stare: I wish I could.
Oh, how I wish I could. Instead, I offer a polite smile to your neighbour

as she starts her story of why she's lying next to you. *Only here because
of Trixie, you know. When those ambulance folk got inside, I was howling*

*fit to burst, for them to find my Trixie. So much pain, Luv, but all I cared
about was that I might have fallen on my little Trixie!*—Yes, Trixie would

not have stood a chance, I ascertain—then I murmur something sympathetic
as I escape to your allotted side of purgatory and pull the screen across.

But she hasn't finished yet. *It was the middle of the night, you know. I was just
getting up for the toilet. Didn't realise that Trixie mustn't have been able to hold*

her bladder too. Then what do you know? I slipped in a puddle of poodle piss!
I take your thin-skinned hand but now you're too distressed; rolling eyes

at your bedside buddy's clearly oft-repeated monologue, and I think to make
a whisper light quip about poor Trixie but decide you're well past the point

of wry or stoic. The woman offers more invisible commentary on the hospital's
selection of digestives, how she prefers assorted cremes, and how her niece

is likely neglecting Trixie while she's stuck in this damn place. Pale and pained
corralled by clatter and chatter, I see you'll have no rest. I sigh and summon

walls, beds, and bodies to crumble into rocks and dust like some big budget
movie scene where only you and I remain, and none shall pass. There, secure

on precipice of laundered linen, sweet air, and solitude, I could serve you peace
or offer waters from the holy lake. This, I'd gladly give, rather than the limp

carnations and lemon drops, untouched on the bedside cabinet. And I'll visit
again tomorrow, then later, back at the nursing home—cocooned in pastel

thoughts, walls, and medically balanced processed care—and wonder what
you'd trade for a mountain top of fresh air, sunshine, and your independence.

Over the Top

She's too much
        too many words
        too many flying fingers
lipstick gasps   fickle highs
and lows
loose lipid streams
        or too loud laughter
wearing imperfections
like a prerogative
        in rooms of clicks   and frowns
when the dress code clearly calls
        for Grace   subdued.

Place a palm upon her knee
        to quieten down
        to keep it in—
those unchecked tremors
beneath skin   push down
        before her colour
                and convictions rise
        her stuck-on-smile
begins to crack   and she stops
        moving with the pack.

Here she comes
        mercurial behind the lens
        beyond the frame
her largeness

like a Coney Island mirror
Munch elongated face
and stretched out moans
jackal cackle   pop-eyed shock
just too much
too over the top.

Best that she now covers up
forgets the past   locks it in
before we see the waddle
beneath chin
that fluster flap of high emotion
enough to name her
negligible
in matters of the final say
those high-pitched cries   all-seeing eyes
must be gagged   and masked
before she takes
her seat at table.

Body of Doubt

Under powder, crème, and cotton, lycra
and the little line of antiperspirant gleam
that licks at fleshy split of arm and breast,
epidermis is warm: while softly—surely
inadequately—holding in a busy throb of
blood, pulse, sinew, padding precious organs,
all squelch and tremble, beneath thin layer
of collected cells, easily pierced by paper,
cat's claws, lies or loathing, even macerated
by many hours sunk in sea. We enfold it all
in cloth and leather, buffer behind steel and
bricks. Walk it round the streets. Rub it up
against each other, awarding smoothest, most
stylish wrappings—prizes; most adored and
most abhorred. And, when it begins to wear
we panic to repaint, retighten, squeeze fat out,
squeeze fat in, pump in chemicals, stimulants
to simulate a blanker stare, smooth plastic glow,
porcelain-capped smile, all to cover what lies
underneath.

Cacophony

I still see words
sparking like struck flint
around your head
when I return to your door
            the ones
you used to thrust like swords
piercing blue
slashing sunny days
to shredded winds
            of cold exhausted trust.

Sting of memory's blade
still picks at scabby layers
of yesterday
            or yet another
            failed tomorrow.
You ranted for years
slept with sorrow
spooned about your back
until you craved its warm
grey breath upon your neck.

Now, I watch you
set your jaw to smiling
as you picture-postcard
us amongst the trees
            with new family
            white painted fence
but at the edges of that frame

one hand in his
the other, stabbing nails
into your palm.

In the grimy distance
            I remember
            ashen cheeks
nights of his stinking yellow
beer, words—combustible as coal.
Now, two lives later—
new husband, house, cut grass—
            you laugh too loudly.
It rattles in my ears
like tin pans.

Colossus

A set of opposable thumbs does not grant me dominion.
  Primates, possums, birds—even some frogs
    could hold cutlery, if so inclined.

I've watched You-Tube stories
  seen raucous Cockatoos raid garbage bins
    claws unclasping our assumptions

as they raise yellow mullets, tough-skinned toes
  in mimicking *stuff-you* salute. Some claim
    there's none as dextrous

who could hope to govern the globe
  but I present to you—the Spider Monkey
    slippery octopus, supposedly domesticated cat.

Aggrandized in effigies as giants who stride
  the sea; colossus legends in our dreams
    reduced to fish-pecked rubble

on a silent ocean floor when earth yawns out
  her slightest shudder. We Yertle ourselves
    to the top of the stack, caring little

for the shells we crack along the climb.
  Views and rule for miles and miles
    yet still we wail at the height of the moon.

How dare it be higher or brighter than us!
the billionaires cry, punching holes into space
just to show that damn universe who's the real boss.

Stick Up

The presidents of America charged into the bank
and let rip with a *ratatatat* of capitalist fire.

Their plastic toothy grins and cut-out eyeholes
dark as bullets determined as destruction

bored into our captured skulls with a calculated
cartoon domination. Forced to kneel we clasped

clammy fingers behind heads whisper-pleading
to the old man with no health insurance *Stay down!*

but he bled out like so much roadkill run down
by wagon trails of followers enroute to serve

their current king. Of course they got away with it
snatching overstuffed bags of stolen sweat and tears

laws stitched and stacked through years and years
while covering tracks to their ivory towers

and arsenals of litigation. Nothing to be done
but lie still and count backwards. When they left

we spat carpet fibres from dry mouths shook off
the shame and shrapnel of defeat reformed

into obedient lines to deposit average yearning
everyday despair and negotiate terms.

Lulu in LA

Still posting
pouts and
dinner plates
at their local
cafes: those
FOMO try-
hards, all so
last year, so
last in line
—cue my
audible eye-
roll—but do
yourself a
favour and
check out the hits on my new channel, *Lulu in LA,*
instead. My slow lorise; luxuriously groomed and
collared tastefully in bling, just has to be the latest
thing. I got one early before demand across the globe

had really taken off. I mean, a
simple otter or Asian water dragon
simply hasn't got the same cachet. I'm
training her to sit at table, maybe even
use a knife and fork. Of course, I've had the
usual jealous commentary claiming she'd be better
off in the forest. Oh, please! My little Lulu, safe from predators, warm and snug in her
monogrammed pyjamas, lapping milk and snacking on smoked salmon from a silver bowl
is truly *#livingherbestlife*. Her diet recommendations were barbaric. Some snowflakes even
try to claim endangerment, babble on about zoonotic
diseases. Whatever! but I swear my Lulu is cleaner
than most people serving me my food. And, by the
way, if you haven't got enough cash to invest in a
replacement, just in case LuLu lost her glow—not
that my baby ever would!— then you shouldn't even
be in the game. Check her out, she's a true sensation!
Make sure to 'like' us and don't forget to subscribe.

Basking

The mogul's getting hitched again
at ninety-three. He can't seem to make one last
past his plans for an afternoon nap
and world domination.

He's obviously outfoxed us all
bought some miraculous elixir
promising another century or two
for him to bask

enjoy the world he's etched
into his own tabloid of alternative
facts and titillation
an empire so layered

in flashy fabrications
that he cannot place
where he left his last wife
or whether he had one at all.

But that cold sharp air
trapped deep within
his hardened throat, dull thud
inside his scaly chest

whoosh and wail of sour sighs
which no physician, pleasure-giver
or employee can relieve
he cannot bear alone.

Each crevice sprawled across his chin
a final line in the sand
        for each bride
        who wasn't what he ordered

                too tall, too much, too mortal
          and maybe too unwilling
          to take that final step
          across the threshold

of a split-tongued forever
hold his hand at each rasping breath
jewelled hand to shrivelled chest
        when darkness comes.

Passing Go

Car chase in New York with the artist formerly known as prince,
his spouse, and splatter of paparazzi, but some claim this was less

pursuit, just more fizz and fluster from a blood-line royal in mid-
transition to Netflix celebrity, embracing new world consciousness

and new world dollars. The comment thread's aflame with curled lip
of daily scorn and the darker shades of loathing, dredged up from

irritable bowels of those crawling bitter spitters. Still, more photos
of that other orange man—his caked-on frowns and smirks ingrained

in a culture now more akin to bacteria growth than customs and beliefs—
prompting me to press palms into eyes and disappear. I could shut down,

pop a pill, pop a tart, pop a shot above the superior orbital rim to feign
insouciance for years and years of unmet yearning. Or maybe, I need

to bring it on, bring my best game, even if it's my worst. As long as it is
loud, proud, and loaded, and I remember what part that I wanted to play,

which token I chose to mark my position. But I can always change my
mind, swap from cat to thimble, iron to boot. It's where you are and where

you're going that really gives you skin. There's no bling if you don't pass
Go. Pity, I'm so wrapped up in the colour and confetti that I forgot to mov

Drive

We cruise along this carbon-breath Freeway
but nothing's ever really free: not tolls,
time, expectations, or the rising cost of clouds,
so sullen in the southern sky. Fuelled
by anticipation, soundtracked on car stereo
to make our average seem grand, traffic—
like our aspirations—slows to barely rolling
crawl. Bloody Volvo drivers who can't merge

and rubber-neckers braking to watch wrecks
of holidays, hiss of fumes from open
bonnets and clenched faces. So, we detour
for a lemon, lime, and bitters at the Maitland
Hotel, where a blue-bruised blonde takes
shaking shots across green felt, her
Alsatian-eyed man standing guard. We
watch, sip silently, then slink back to the car.

Another album please. You hate the way I touch
CDs with my french fry fingers, fret over
your possessions around my careless hands. I hate
the way you speed round corners, holding
threats of kangaroos or feral children. We share
a Ploughman's Lunch in a gauzed verandah,
drink the first red; *Hill of Hope*, aptly chosen
for our first weekend away, see sky divers

land before blackening clouds. First drops fall,
raise dust, then water hardens into hail.

You like my denim overalls: let hands waterfall
  down their open sides. Pulse quickens on
the drive to find the nearest vacancy. This motel
  will do. And it does. Late for breakfast
so, we're served defeated bacon, cold eggs,
  but we hardly care. Under stoic sky, we drive,

in search of horses. Past lazy hills, wild fields,
  and gum scent, tires climb a crumbly road to *Silver
Bridles*. Scratching dog ears, fence post leaning
  for an hour until horses are girthed and saddled.
Resigned to her chore, a roan mare swipes
  green drool across your new shirt. You feign
nonchalance—badly—while horse titters, I clutch
  reins, and try to hide my grin. Trotting behind

the boss horse, you flail, determined to stay on horse.
  Bless your well-laundered cotton socks.
Twilight washed paddocks drift past the passenger
  window. Cows stare and chew and my mood
darkens, as it does. Your whistling irritates, angle
  of your chin and suddenly, I want no more of you,
but by the time we gravel-crunch down an olive
  tree driveway to arrive at the next guesthouse—

sweet apple-pear pie, strong coffee in the cedar
  scented conservatory—we sway back into the crisp
fresh thrill of each other again. Avocado, and corn
  fritters for our last breakfast then back into
the car, sliding down that hill of hope we'd climbed
  and into smoky city cares again. Alone, in
my mismatched sheet bed and mixed-up head,
  lips still tingling of you, I question everything.

Man Beneath the Mountain

In the old world
when his breath seared
strong, yet not enough
to burn a city, he still
wore skin, bled crimson
for his pain and walked
among us. Now, in times
uncertain: emerald eye
scouring all, he rolls a
boulder—huge, hermetic—
across the entrance to
his mountain lair, claws
atop his hoard of gleam
and glory, exhales a final
smoky sigh, sweeps
third eye-lid clean
of glint and shimmer
before he takes his rest.

Servants stationed
at the gates to warn
of fortress breach, while
outside storms and mortal
howls become mere whispers
on the breeze he's trapped
inside his vast and air-
conditioned halls.
Eyes closed tight, he still
sees: moves through

memory, well-paid soldiers
fortifying loopholes,
sealing tunnels watertight
with labyrinths of legal
machinations, all to preserve
his mythological might.
For, there's always some
deluded knight who tries
to wake the sleeping giant.

But legends don't lose sleep
over casual incineration.
We warm work-hardened
hands around small fires,
share tales of struggle,
dark days of need,
and wish for saviours.
His power—wings that span
our world in shadows—
could build, restore, and yet
he reaps and reaps.

Rupture

Breath breaks
closes like a fist inside his lungs
as he plunges into
blue-green skin of deep
bends torso, thrusts feet
into a loose-limbed splutter
bubbles, silt, and leaving
in his wake.

He is seeking treasure
seeking the submerged
yet still unknown: something
silver, sharp or mythical
to illuminate his too-dark world
so thick with seaweed and secrets
blur of movement
slip of tail

and the cold briny horror
of imagined teeth, barnacled
fingers snatching from below.
Silence prickles ears and nose
as he rams resistance
but water: its liquid palm
heavy as lead, presses head
forcing back

when fingers, like small
fishes, probe too far.

Laboured kicks won't breach
the lock of bubbled deep.
Chest bursting with surrender
he gasps to surface
once more betrayed,
but buoyant.

How to Prosper From the Fall

'...the fundamental weakness of Western civilisation is empathy....' *Elon Musk Feb 28, 2025*

If you don't pull by the roots, he said,
then it's just rip and cut back, shred and pluck.
You'll only curb a little wild, waste
another season when time to cull is finally ripe.

So much easier to plough and fell, take
a chainsaw to the trunk; its fifty spreading
branches, and hollow out an age-ringed
constitution. Pay no heed to howls

or splinters, crack and cleave of living
timber, swarms of soft blind parasites
that scuttle from the hacks. Inhale, instead,
the musky scent of smoking blade,

the well-oiled spin and endless thrum
of our invincible machine. Then, when
rare earth is stripped and fallow, make sure
to cultivate so only what you feed will grow.

Some faith and flowers may be lost,
but wealth and power guaranteed.
Imagine: one pure soil, one seed to share
among the chosen reapers. Focus only

on the price and yield a righteous raze
and replant wields. Hold up your bloody
dirt-stained hand, high as a kite, in vile
salute to make yourself feel great again.

Seraphim's Last Song

Miss Navarro won't let us crawl
under desks during maths.
She never says 'shit' or lets spit
stream down her chin, but now
she's fallen over Michael
in the reading corner and both
are leaking red and still as stone.

I'm leaking too: legs piss-sticky,
wobbling like birthday jelly
while I crouch level with two dirty
Nikes stomping past my table.
Smell of sharpenings, farts and
something like burnt rubber,
boom in my ears, blood

on my tongue, heart hurting
in my chest and scream stuck
in my neck as I wish
for wings. Gabriel's head is open,
like his eyes. I squeeze mine
shut so all I see is Mom.
She'll have to wash my pants.
I can't go to Little League like this

and we won't win the final
if Michael cannot move because
he's our best striker. Raphael
is crying too loudly next to me.

I think of that thing Dad said
the day he brought home bullets
for the pistol locked beside his bed

Guns don't kill people; people do
but here's this gun busting bodies
in my classroom and now
it's pointed straight at me.

III

I Cannot Build a Shelter

from hollow sticks in the grass
snapped with cold fingers broken
with boot crunched by the claws
of brush turkey feet hurled skyward
in storm and too damp to burn
too fickle too thin to build shield
from the wind that might thatch
a tense weave against chill of the night.
The song of the birds cannot build me
a bridge a ladder of notes to climb
out of my grief or a shawl of sweet
twitters to lull me to sleep. The rustle
of leaves will not cluster a cover
to keep out the rain hard hail of words
blister of sun and when doubt's six-
leg scuttle crawls over soft skin
I cannot brush it off with a thicket
of stars plucked down from the black.
Hands will not warm by the flame
of red poppies glowing good night
in the shadow of dusk and I will not
prove wisdom from passage of time
falling white like the snow upon
my greying hair etching frowns
strumming taut over memories and sighs
I'd much rather forget the meanness
the part of my soul that seems set
into lines about lips—limits of grace.

But I will build shelter within these small
words   a home for my yearning   layered
in script   sealed in dry ink   patched
with hubris and hope   wrapping heart
with the wishes of how it could be
building story and scene   to pad
bones and belief   and assemble
a shelter   from sharps and debris.

Urban Birdsong

One's still asleep, the other
pounding over Harbour Bridge
in his new Christmas runners.

I lean into right hip, the way
the physio warned was a bad habit,
stare into morning, gifted

like crinkled pastel sheets
of tissue paper, unfolding blue
from open concertina doors.

A few optimistic fruit flies
hover over scraps spilt
from the pedal bin. Screech
of trucks,

A distant shout.
Honking horns. Maybe a siren
but only me before this open balcony.

Faint scent of frangipani
on the breeze softens
last night's remnants of fried onion.

Cabbage moth meanders over trees
settles briefly on blossom and green
then floats across another canvas.

Yap of dog in nearby courtyard
traffic-chopper buzz, somewhere
 a pneumatic drill

creak of upstairs floorboards
neighbour's turning faucets
boiling water, beginning

or ending things.
But it's all out there
beyond doors, streets, clouds

glint and clatter simply background
to these solitary moments
sipping tea, breathing start of day.

On Norton Street

I see Michelangelo arms
hung loose from open car windows
    solid firm sienna-kissed
catching the fingers of god or gravel.
Shadowed jaws thrust in time
to the bass boom beat
fading past the traffic lights.

    I used to live here
    in a paint-peeling semi
and the petrol station brothers
just a few doors up called me, *Katarina*
when I'd rush in for milk bread
    or chocolate bars when there used to be
a petrol station and a Polynesian nightclub
cross the street. The fanciest restaurant
back then now seems small and grey
even its water fountain looks tired.

Now buildings squeeze
    against each other
pushing to be the brightest
most authentic to the motherland.
    In the balcony-tiered Forum
we inhale alfresco smells
tomato herbs cheese and coffee
persuading us we're Vespa-scooting Romans
    rather than the smoky refugees
    from Parramatta Road.

Prove Humanity

Check a box
to prove you're not a box
of whirring parts
wired circuits or stuff
you just don't understand
but still, you have to
check a box
until they teach the box
and bots to understand
then when the box
learns to recognise
our patterns, ways
that we read street signs
identify green from amber
traffic lights, cursive
script from blurred
all those things
that CAPTCHA
our imperfections
slow scroll uncertainties
then they'll have to
set the sentient
new challenges—like
state whether the emperor
dons a blonde or orange
hairpiece (if he's wearing
one at all) or whether
genocide is simply
military method

sanctioned by belief
—to prove your
own humanity.

Chiaroscuro

After a charcoal drawing 'Midlife' by Anne Cape

I.

All clear ahead,
peripheral—just shadow shapes
and things to worry about
tomorrow. Chin-tilted toward
imminence, daring days to take the best
of youth: the quick-twitch bound,
lithe nonchalance, a ready laugh
and satisfying pump of expectation.
Straight-backed, sure,
yet hotly reckless, we race hours,
squander gold and bluebird days,
too preoccupied with Coney-Island
mirror views of full-cheeked,
full-of-self distortions.

Imbibing possibility,
we hurdle turnstyles, fist to sky,
tongue to skin and sweat to salt,
each cut glass moment, eye upon the prize
that we're not even sure we want.
Risk and faith coursing through
our thin-walled veins like chalice wine:
            you, child, are blessed,
each fall, another channel
into grace.

II.

But now, we blend in shadow.
Span of days are brown and clay,
mortgage mauved, rust-edged
with average—
sandwich crusts, stiff knees,
too many waiting rooms,
a building throb in upper temple
          tick ticking, calling time
to discard what was never
reached, the weight of sighs,
the great unsaid.

Travellers

Sifting back through days when flesh still yearned
for flesh: wine-breathed, warm-skinned,
bursting for touch—
            that night we couldn't wait,
sand scraping thighs, full
moon, black ocean pounding
in our ears

            but now we wane; moon-gazing
from car windows, dripping
into wickless shapes
of working days, wholemeal
bread, and long-forgotten wishes.
            Those lovers on the beach
look less like us each year

yet, still, you stay
my keeper of secrets and forgiveness:
discarding all those spit-stained
moments, times I didn't win
            the room, the job, the day
and watched me fling excuses into echoes,
rebounding over years.

On and on, we chafe and fluster,
so familiar with each other's rusty
ways—scraped toast, cold
hands, a dirty sink, the same old
stories told to friends—

all ebb and flow
of our beloved moanings.

We've arrived at where we never thought
we'd land: more likely to have parted
at the fork, held out a wistful hand
in waving silhouette then faded
into distance. This destination:
one, we never bought a ticket for,
still somehow, feels like home.

Slush

Who popped your literary cherry
for your first time—
first call to spill it to the page

a tick of *yes*, a taste of *that's the spot*
and jiggled your submission
like a tassled titty, right back at you

with a lofty editorial smile
and been-around-the-block advice
for first time users: *maybe*

build a little slower, tone it down
a bit, no need to give it all away
but panting through

your sloppy selection gratitude
still flows the desperate rush
to *work it, baby, work it.*

And did you own it like a boss?
squeeze those thirsty verbs
and awkward lineations

into taut pulsating rhythms
so they might get their minute's
slot up on the slippery pole?

Or did you miss out once again
still dressed off trend
your too-large pores, clumsy

stanza twerks, just not enough
            or way too much
graceless bump and grind

to make your words
worth price of admission?
All those extended metaphors

blow-hard polemics
festering in the pile. Find your
voice, my wide-eyed wannabe

give it air and give it edge
            and remember
we're all talking to ourselves

Picnic on Observatory Hill

The rotunda—trust the poets to debate the name—
            Gazebo? someone murmured
            maybe a summerhouse   or arbour?
Name the platform what you will
but stretched out over picnic rugs
seated on the stone arc of the Boer War
Memorial or queuing patiently to recite
—at least louder than birds and cheering
bridal parties wandering through words—
writers gathered at the skirts of her high sides.

Chasing a coquettish sun to cheat the chill
of September shadows we shifted blankets
squinted at voices, verse devoured by laughter
gush of breeze and rumblings of trains.
Into the squawk and celebration of the day
the mic persisted—at times a burst of stronger
phrase, then low and lulling as the soft
honey hues of a sinking sun.

The literary lingered with their peculiar
purpleness, earnestness, and longing
while Tug: in comedic casual control
lifted a wry eyebrow at the enormous *Bearly*
There teddy bear and balloon display below—
            a gender reveal in full throttle finery
            silks, stilettos—and all oblivious
to the slightly amused man reciting poems above.

Then someone mused on Megan Markle
            someone lived alone with cats
            someone mocked the payment of poems
and seriously, it was too hard to hear much else.
A partner, sent on corkscrew duty, retrieved
one from a group of more practical poets
who recognised the contemporary ridiculousness
of corks but who'd come armed anyway.

The poetry support spouses chatted
about bridges, battle strategies in Ukraine
while we slathered forth to spill glasses, souls
with our fellow afflicted: licking wounds
about lack of inspiration, publishers, or publication.
And, for the Finale, just when we thought
the Poet's Picnic might meander back
            to things more philosophical

a grinning quad of slick suited men
joined our emcee, mid-poem, upon the balcony
to shoot pink dust blasts into late afternoon
and boisterously declare
the happy couple's girlish hopes.
While poets, all flushed with wine and pride
—such opportunists, scavengers all—
chose simply to applaud
            and believe our words
            were finally given due fanfare.

Lunchbox

Long days of chalk dust, parched earth
playgrounds: our hands—sugar sticky
          or caked in dried up Clag paste
          from Sister Ursula's latest craft idea—
                    would grasp and cling as we upended,
                    bloomers blaring from the monkey bars,

          while Sister shrieked,
          palm to chest in high-pitched horror
          at such bold display,
          unladylike behaviour.

          Young girls were supposed to sit
          still   cross-ankled
          after nibbling their devon sandwiches
          and recite the rosary,
                    eyes raised to heaven,
                    as they massaged the beads
                              of Christ's luminous glory

or sip from sun-baked bottles
left out at little lunch to build up bones:
          white milk, curdled yellow
          like a snarl of small-town bigotries,
          and likely not on offer
          to the *Tulladunna* camp kids—
                    most unseen or unenrolled.

A swift swipe on the knuckles
for colouring outside the lines,
subtracting incorrectly or getting caught
with cake-stall toffee
stashed beneath your desk
        cause dibber-dobber Stuart told again.

But it was last term Friday afternoons
that took out childhood's biggest prize—
        splashing in the council pool,
        no lessons, lifeguards, sunscreen,
        just slippery tiles and too much chlorine,
                my hair; green-tipped blonde all summer.

Then, towelled and combed,
we'd clutch coins, flick and shove
        to purchase musk sticks, Sunny Boys,
        sherbet fizz   tingling on tongues
                the whole long bus ride home.

Naming Animals

You don't need a map, you say—
            can recognise exhibits
                        replicate the sounds
match colours with the pictures
perused so many years by bedside lamp.

It's true, no guardian's needed
at the zoo, once you've come of age
                once teeth are down
not wisdom, but at least, incisors
sharp enough for biting.

You used to call crocs, *snappydiles*
            and sang to them of never smiling
while I gripped your T-shirt tight
in case you leaned towards their pit
            but I can't hold much longer.

So, welcome to feeding time
            where hoof by hide and snarl
by growl, softer souls with softer
skins are shoved aside
            until the trough is almost dry.

            I know I always taught you
            wait your turn
but once the pen is open—run, child, run.
The wild take what they want
and give no quarter.

You think the keeper will save you?
Their shots are aimed to quell
not to assist.
            I'd like to tell you; take your time
view a while, watch the ways

the creatures swing and sway
note twitch of ears and hackles rise
before you sign up for the muck out—
            believe me, there'll be time
            for shovelling shit—

                        but you've already run ahead
                        and brushed aside my hand.

On Reflection

That mirror woman doesn't look like me.
Shadows squat in slopes of cheeks

jaw slouching with the weight
of sighs. She wears years

like a hospital gown: shapeless, plain
to cover up bare truths.

Captured in the escalator glass
reflected in the Woolworths window

or a soft-skinned cashier's required
smile, she blurs into background

anonymous as a headless statue
metamorphic under pressure

and hardened to hold average
aspirations within

her blue-veined marbled grasp.
From a cardboard box of way-back-when

I've saved decades, days
selected effigies of who I thought

I was: polished versions of the past
that might console the mirror woman.

How pretty in that blue dress
such trim waist, such slender fingers

which the cafeteria lady
grabbed one day to hold up to a friend

Look! This one's never done
a real day's work!

Now, the mirror woman's hands
are worn and whorled as tree trunks

and even though her frown and frizzled hair
look nothing like that blue-dress girl

she's enduring as an ancient sculpture
beautiful, beyond the ruin.

Warm Brew

Black leaf in boiling
water always made
it better: a little milk,
hands cupped around
warm crockery as we
sat knee to knee on
kitchen stools, nursing
average disappointment
and small satisfactions.
Never too sweet: poured
out once turning tepid
or too weak, and boiled
again, the simple brew
brought us to the table
with a reason to stop
and sip, give minutes,
hours to each other and
share a Scotch Finger,
stories, or a weighty sigh
across Laminex benches,
kettle whistle afternoons
or still black mornings;
awake too early, too alone.
You didn't need a pot
when a teabag would do
and drank enough to drown
a small village along the
Indian ocean. And even
though, after each visit

I would drive off, bloated
as a toad, I could never
refuse the offer of another
cup. It would be like saying
no to a piece of your heart.

Into the Forest

If you ever want to find my mother
follow the tissues:
those crumpled,
hardly damp, thin cotton clouds
held to twitching lips,
nervous nostrils, spilling from pockets,
sleeves or shaking fingers
when she's clutching a cup of tea
or remnants of her dignity.

Like an ancient Gretel,
she's still leaving trails,
flagging out her one-way journey
into deeper woodlands,
losing pieces of herself
along the darkening path,
but signalling the past
to light the way.
Sometimes it does.
Sometimes
a shred of memory
floats briefly to ground;

a verse of song, a long-lost
name, remembered
tale, faint tang of ginger,
before they're tucked
or thrown away.

She's stashed them
into cardigans or creases
of her brown recliner chair.
They tail her like tame white mice
nibbling at heels,
fussing about familiar things,
all furry scuttle
and whiskered kiss,
but unintelligible
as forgotten secrets,
years of unanswered
questions.

She must have them close—
these soft scrunched
papers of the past,
touching, mopping
all that drips
and slips away.

Believe

Birds do not believe in clouds,
they soar straight through—
damp feathered and derisive
of the emptiness soft-held
in all those water vapour clusters
feigning fat white lies.

That's maybe why so many
shatter: stunned or broken
beside windows, doors of glass,
squawking at deceptions, our love
of invisible things, and nests built
brick by bone of bartered hours

and sold souls. Now, her dot sticker
eyes and open, closing beak
on the other side of the pane
seem to accuse: *Liars, liars, all.*
I used to believe in clouds
until the roar of a Boeing 737

dissolved my Kinder innocence,
back when I'd paint stick-figure
me and stick-figure you
floating in a bright blue sky.
Yet, while reason reminds
there is nothing above,

nothing to hold in the heavens,
I believe—like ice crystals
suspended in the atmosphere—
you too, are somewhere,
a misty kiss upon my cheek
or shiver of a brisk new dawn.

Dominion

"...the depth closed me round about, the weeds were wrapped about my head." Jonah 2:5

What did Jonah know: entombed in warm, black
belly—down deep—weeds wrapped about his wilful
head, keeling body and regret into an expected end?

Beyond his shock reprieve—yawned rupture
of those massive jaws, a spumous, bold ejection
into second life—did he shudder, weep or wail,

praise the random wonder of the natural world
or claim prophecy and creed? The whales knew.
Once, these giants may have walked the land,

hind legs slowly shrinking over thirty million
years. Before the testaments of man, before we
claimed dominion, it was theirs. Foresaw when

to ease the earth, glide their growing forms into
the sea, knew we were unprepared for deep; could
not discern their dirge-like songs or echo revelations.

Imagine they return—heave their massive, round,
smooth sides ashore, sway through bracken, lurch
through cities and belief—to swallow whole again.

Notes

'Invocation': Mary Albert of the Bardi people tells the story of how Australian native birds got their bright feathers, and why the crow stayed black.

'Records of Ephemera': *A People's Archive of Sinkng and Melting* is a collection of materials contributed by people living in places that may disappear because of the combined physical, political, and economic impacts of climate change, primarily sea level rise, erosion, desertification, and glacial melting. http://www.sinkingandmelting.org/

'LaNiña': The 'Never Never' is the name of a vast, remote area of the Australian Outback, as described in Barcroft Boake's poem 'Where the Dead Men Lie'.

'Cold Hard Truths': In the late 1980s, Australia and France led a push for an international environmental treaty covering Antarctica called the Madrid Protocol. Treaty parties were required to clean up abandoned work and waste sites where it can be done without creating more environmental harm than leaving it in place. Today, environmental risks still remain from hazards posed by abandoned sites.

'Meeting my Edge': Globally, it is estimated that 5% of adults suffer from depression (World Health Organisation)

Acknowledgements

Special thanks to both the Round Table Poets (NSW) and the Arboretum Poets (ACT) for their generous advice, feedback and inspiration. A particular thank you to Margaret Bradstock for her informal mentorship and to Denise O'Hagan for wonderful conversations and friendship. Also, a shout-out to Shane Strange for his tireless commitment to poetry and publishing. A patient and insightful editor.

Poems have appeared or are forthcoming in the following Australian and International journals and anthologies:

Cordite, StylusLit, Rochford St Review, Rabbit, Australian Poetry Journal, fourW, Splinter, Authora Australis, Other Terrain, ACU Poetry Prize Anthology 2023, Liquid Amber Award Anthology 2023, If Writing Were a Cure: the 2024 UC Health Poetry Prize, Grieve: Hunter Writers' Centre Anthology 2022, and 2024, Ros Spencer Award: Brushstrokes Anthology 2023, Chroma: South Coast Writer's Centre Anthology 2023, Telling Australia's Truth Anthology: Ginninderra 2023, Poetry d'Amour Anthology WA 2024, Cows: Pure Slush, Skylight 47 (Ireland), *The Bangor Literary Review* (Ireland), *ROPES Literary Journal* (Ireland), *The Martello (Ireland), The Broken Spine* (UK), *Confluences* (UK), *London, Grip* (UK), *The Threepenny Review* (USA), *Sheepshead Review* (USA), *Stone Poetry Quarterly* (USA), *Quartet* (USA), *Moria* (USA), *Arboreal* (USA), *Heimat Review* (USA), *Live Encounters* (Indonesia), *The Wild Word* (Germany), *The Amphibian* (Netherlands).

Poems have been commended, shortlisted, or longlisted in the following prizes:

'Into the Forest' awarded an *In Memoriam Award Prize* in the *Grieve: Hunter Writers' Centre Anthology 2024.*

'The Forest and the Trees' and 'Warm Brew' were shortlisted in *the ACU Poetry Prize Anthology 2023*
'Meeting my Edge' shortlisted in the *UC Health Poetry Prize 2024*
'Urban Birdsong' was Highly Commended in the *Kyogle Readers and Writers Competition 2023*
'Kaleidoscope' Longlisted in the *Liquid Amber Award Anthology 2023*
'One Cool Evening in May' commended in the *Lambing Flat, Young FAW Writing Competition, 2023*

About the Author

Kate Maxwell was born in the small country town of Wee Waa. She has spent most of her life as a Sydney resident but is now acclimatizing to the different pace and temperature of Canberra. Kate is a teacher, poet, and short story writer. She has been published and awarded in many Australian and International literary magazines such as *Cordite, Rabbit, Splinter, The Galway Review,* and *The Threepenny Review*. Kate has been nominated for best micro fiction on the Net in 2021 and best short fiction in 2023. *Thistle* is her third poetry collection. Her earlier collections are *Never Good at Maths* (Interactive Publications, 2021) and *Down the Rabbit Hole* (Ginninderra, 2023). Kate's interests include film, wine, and sleeping.

Find her at https://kateswritingplace.com/

www.ingramcontent.com/pod-product-compliance
Ingram Content Group Australia Pty Ltd
76 Discovery Rd, Dandenong South VIC 3175, AU
AUHW020611080726
429626AU00003B/5

9 781764 106870